2 Minutes and Under
VOLUME 2

2 Minutes and Under
VOLUME 2

More Original
Character Monologues
for Actors

Glenn Alterman

MONOLOGUE AUDITION SERIES

A Smith and Kraus Book

Published by Smith and Kraus, Inc.
177 Lyme Road, Hanover, NH 03755
www.SmithKraus.com

First Edition: November 2002
10 9 8 7 6 5 4 3
Manufactured in the United States of America

Cover and text design by Julia Hill Gignoux, Freedom Hill Design

Library of Congress Cataloguing-in-Publication Data
Alterman, Glenn, 1946–
2 minutes and under 2 : character monologues for actors /
Glenn Alterman. —1st ed.
p. cm.
ISBN 1-57525-324-0
1. Monologues. 2. Acting. [1. Monologues. 2. Acting-Auditions.]
I. Title. II. Title: 2 minutes and under 2.
PN2080.A443   2002
812'.54—dc21   2002030915

THE AUTHOR

GLENN ALTERMAN is the author of *2 Minutes and Under, Street Talk: Original Character Monologues for Actors, Uptown, The Job Book: One Hundred Acting Jobs for Actors, The Job Book 2: One Hundred Day Jobs for Actors, What to Give Your Agent For Christmas, 2-Minute Monologues, Creating Your Own Monologue,* and *Promoting Your Acting Career: An Actor's Guide to Making It In New York City.*

2 Minutes and Under, Street Talk, Uptown, Creating Your Own Monologue, both volumes of *The Job Book,* and *Promoting Your Acting Career: An Actor's Guide to Making It In New York City* were all featured selections in The Doubleday Book Club (Fireside Theater and Stage And Screen Division"). Most of his published works have gone on to multiple printings.

His plays *Like Family* and *The Pecking Order* were recently optioned by Red Eye Films (with Alterman writing the screenplay).

His latest play, *Solace,* was produced off-Broadway by Circle East Theater Company and presently has several European productions. *Solace* was recently optioned for European TV.

Nobody's Flood won the Bloomington National Playwriting Competition as well as being a finalist in the Key West Playwriting Competition.

Coulda-Woulda-Shoulda won the Three Genres Playwriting Competition twice (including publication of the play in two separate editions of the Prentice-Hall college textbook). It has received several New York productions.

He wrote the book for *Heartstrings—The National Tour* (commissioned by the Design Industries Foundation For Aids), a thirty-five city tour that starred Michelle Pfeiffer, Ron Silver, Christopher Reeve, Susan Sarandon, Marlo Thomas, and Sandy Duncan.

Other plays include *Kiss Me When It's Over* (commissioned by E. Weissman Productions) starring and directed by Andre DeShields,

Tourists of the Mindfield (finalist in the L. Arnold Weissberger Playwriting Competition at New Dramatists), and *Street Talk/Uptown* (based on his monologue books), produced at the West Coast Ensemble. *Goin' Round on Rock Solid Ground, Unfamiliar Faces,* and *Words Unspoken* were all finalists at the Actor's Theater of Louisville. *Spilt Milk* received its premiere at the Beverly Hills Rep/Theater 40 in Los Angeles and was selected to participate in the Samuel French One-Act Festival. It's had over twenty productions, including most recently with Emerging Artists Theater Company in New York. *The Danger of Strangers* won Honorable Mention in the Deep South Writers Conference Competition, the Pittsburgh New Works Festival and was also a finalist in the George R. Kernodle Contest. There have been over fifteen productions, including Circle Rep Lab, the West Bank Downstairs Theater Bar (starring James Gandolphini), the Emerging Artists Theater Company's One-Act Marathon, and most recently at the Vital Theater Company on Theater Row in New York.

His work has been performed at Primary Stages, Circle in the Square Downtown, the Turnip Festival, HERE, LaMama, at the Duplex, Playwrights Horizons, at several theaters on Theater Row in New York, as well as at many other theaters around the country.

He is one of the country's foremost monologue and audition coaches, having helped thousands of actors in their search and preparation of monologues, as well as creating their own material for solo shows.

Glenn has lectured and taught at such diverse places as the Edward Albee Theater Conference (Valdez, Alaska), Southampton College, Governors School For the Arts (Old Dominion University), the School For Film and Television, Western Connecticut State College, Star Map Acting School of Long Island, the Dramatists Guild, the Learning Annex, the Screen Actors Guild, the Seminar Center, in the Boston Public School System, as well as at many acting schools all over the country.

In 1994 he created the Glenn Alterman Studio (glennalterman.com) and through its auspices has worked privately as a monologue/audition coach and at colleges, universities, and acting schools all around the country. He presently lives in New York City where he writes plays and screenplays.

ACKNOWLEDGMENTS

Glenn Alterman wishes to thank the following people for their help in the development of these monologues: Leslie H. Raskin, Circle East Theater Company (Michael Warren Powell, Artistic Director) Emerging Artists Theater Company (Paul Adams, Artistic Director, Jonathan Reunning, literary director), Jimmy Georgiades, Scotty Bloch, Kit Flannigan, Anna Ewing Bull, Nelson Avidon, Wynne Anders, Carter Inskeep, Judy Hiller, Jim Ireland, Nell Mooney, Delphi Harrington, Robert Groder, Blanche Cholet, Rachel Lee Harris, Rebecca Hoodwin, Ed Moran, Jeff Riebe, Chris Weikel, Meg Anderson, Katie Carol, Elaine Rinehart, and of course, Eric Kraus, Marisa Smith, and the staff at Smith and Kraus Publishers.

DEDICATION

This book is dedicated to the people of the City of New York. And to the actors who come to New York to pursue their dreams. May their dreams and the lights on Broadway never dim.

Table of Contents

Foreword xiii

WOMEN

Vera, twenty and older, Dramatic 2
    a young executive who walked away from a prestigious job
Chloe, twenty-five and older, Comedic 4
    a woman who finally gets a date with the guy she's been
    dreaming about for years
Mary, thirty and older, Dramatic 6
    a religious woman with a very unusual job
Melanie, any age, Comedic. 7
    a woman who is addicted to sales
Henrietta, fifty-five and older, Serio-comedic. 9
    a long time married woman discussing why her husband shot her
Gwyneth, teens to early twenties, Comedic 11
    an inexperienced actress terrified at an audition
Betty, any age, Serio-comedic 15
    a woman tells off her boyfriend
Yvonne, any age, Serio-comedic. 17
    a mom talks about her baby boy
Linda-Anne, any age, Dramatic 18
    a woman recalling the last time she saw her enraged father
Harriet, any age, Comedic 20
    a sexually active woman who has just freaked out
Thelma, fifty and older, Dramatic. 21
    a grandmother lovingly remembering her grandson
Angela, adult, Comedic 22
    a tough Italian housewife
Annie-May, late teens to early twenties, Serio-comedic. 24
    a young girl recalling a terrifying date

Karen, any age, Dramatic 26
    a terrified airplane passenger

Kit, senior citizen, Serio-comedic 27
    a woman who recently fled from a retirement home

Bernice Weinstein, thirty and older, Comedic. 29
    a wife lambasting her husband for not being able to find
    the ketchup

Tina, adult, Comedic. 31
    a hostess seducing one of her dinner guests

Sadie, fifty and older, Dramatic 34
    a woman remembering her strict mother

Gloria, any age, Dramatic 35
    a woman who has just caught her husband having sex
    with someone

Cynthia, forty and older, Serio-comedic 37
    a wife recalling her early family life

Stephanie, adult, Dramatic 38
    a bar patron looking out the window

Sybil, forty and older, Dramatic. 39
    a mother telling her son about his father

Marcia, any age, Serio-comedic 40
    a woman who has just had a health scare

Anita, a young mom, Dramatic 42
    a mom recalling a terrifying incident with her baby

Venetia, thirty and older, Dramatic 44
    a wife telling off her husband

Ina, any age, Dramatic 45
    a woman at an intervention

Netti, adult, Dramatic. 46
    a woman reunited with her sister

Grace, twenties to thirties, Comedic. 47
    a neurotic woman declaring her independence

Ellen, any age, Serio-comedic. 48
    a woman who ran over a man with her car

Myriam, twenties to forties, Dramatic 50
a woman trying to get rid of the man she just had sex with

MEN

Herm, any age, Dramatic 52
a man who passionately loves Julia
Len, adult, Comedic 54
a man joyfully recalls his first
Ronald, adult, Serio-comedic 56
an ex-con
Harold, adult, Dramatic 57
a man recalling a childhood memory
Memphis, adult, Dramatic 58
a homeless man who just witnessed a murder
Stan, adult, Serio-comedic 60
*a man who was once going to be a preacher recalls the day
he lost his faith*
Mickey, fifty and older, Dramatic 62
a drag queen preparing for his act
Timothy, any age, Comedic 63
an employee at a prestigious company
John, any age, Dramatic 65
a recently rescued man
Henry, any age, Serio-comedic 66
an artist confronting a fellow artist
Murray, adult, Serio-comedic 69
a teacher lecturing about the commandment, "Love thy parents"
Neil, forty and older, Serio-comedic 71
a man recalling a drunken night with his buddy
Don, any age, Dramatic 73
any age, a son recalling the effect his fathers leaving had on his life
Hamilton, any age, Dramatic 74
a son remembering how he stole money from his mother

Jay, adult, Serio-comedic 76
    a man discussing his infidelity
Jack, adult, Dramatic 77
    a gay man remembering his best friend
Bart, any age, Comedic 79
    a subway rider recalling an erotic encounter on the subway
Josh, adult, Dramatic 81
    a man recalling an experience in a Jewish synagogue
Richard, adult, Dramatic. 83
    a gay man recalling an early sexual encounter
Mike, adult, Comedic 85
    an abusive husband
Michael, any age, Dramatic. 87
    a man telling his brother he has Aids
Jeremy, any age, Dramatic. 88
    a father saying good night to his son
Murray, adult, Serio-comedic. 90
    a teacher of Judiasm lectures about God
Seymour, middle-aged and older, Dramatic. 92
    a loving husband remembers his wife
Brian, any age, Comedic 93
    a dad who just had a baby
Ned, adult, Dramatic 95
    a patient discussing a memory about his mother with his therapist
Gary, any age, Dramatic 97
    a grieving husband
Sam, adult, Serio-comedic 99
    a dad recalls the birth of his son
Mark, adult, Comedic. 101
    a man obsessed with a woman he recently met at a club

Foreword

An audition monologue is a marketing tool. Its main purpose is to help get you an acting job or an agent. But finding just the right monologue can be a very frustrating experience. Believe me, I know, I've been there. When I was actively pursuing acting, I'm sure I logged in hundreds of hours going through plays, monologue books, and movie scripts searching for that "perfect piece." I wanted a monologue that had an engaging story, a beginning, middle, and end, emotions I could relate to, a character I wanted to play, and a journey I was willing to take. Finding a monologue that met all those criteria, I discovered, was a daunting experience. So, out of my frustration I decided to write my own audition monologue. I let my imagination guide me, and somehow, after much trial and error, I turned out a pretty good piece. I tried it out in acting class and received a very enthusiastic response. That first monologue led to a whole new career for me. I began writing monologues with a fervor; all types, all kinds. At first, just for myself, and later on for fellow actors. Writing audition monologues has been the main focus of my writing career for over eleven years now. I was recently dubbed "The Monologue Man" in a newspaper article discussing my work. After all these years I still find each new monologue to be an exciting challenge, a new adventure. And I still get a charge whenever I see an actor give a knock-out audition with one of my pieces. All in all I suppose I've written well over four hundred audition monologues. Many of them appear in my five published books of monologues (most of them with Smith and Kraus).

The monologues for *2 Minutes and Under Volume 2* were put through a tough developmental process utilizing the actors, directors, and playwrights of two theater companies, Circle East and Emerging Artists. Aside from my own personal assessment, I listened to any feedback from company members. Then after I did the rewrites, I sent the monologues off to several casting directors I work with for their opinions. Only the monologues that survived these rigorous screenings made the cut. I'm extremely proud of the monologues in this book. I honestly believe that even if you're as discerning as I am that you'll find at least a few monologues within these pages to your liking. Have a browse, see if any of the characters touch you, engage you, speak to you.

Auditioning can be very stressful, we all know that. But one way to alleviate at least some of the stress is going into that audition room with a monologue that you just can't wait to perform. I've also included in the book a group of one-minute monologues for those auditions that request them, and some longer ones.

At this time I'd like to sincerely thank all the actors who have contacted me over the years to express their appreciation for my work. It's a great feeling to know that something you've written has touched people and the same time helped them in their careers. I wish you all the best of luck and hope that you succeed in all your dreams.

Glenn Alterman, May 11, 2002, New York City

Women's
Monologues

VERA
twenty and older
Dramatic

Vera tells her best friend why she walked away from a top position in a prestigious corporation.

I walked away, simple. I mean it really didn't mean that much to me. You have no idea what it was like. What it feels like, Martha, to wake up every morning and know that just because you're in charge, your day will be filled with deceit, lies, and larceny. And because you're young and new, people assume you're innocent and naïve. And so games get played, lessons are learned; survival. And overnight it seems, you develop fangs, mistrust. And in a matter of months, Martha, it seems everyone you meet is a potential enemy, starting with the bagel boy in the morning. And every meeting you take becomes a minefield. So you tiptoe everywhere, try not to breathe too deeply, talk too loud, and not think a thought that might be "misinterpreted." You're a woman, a threat, and your every action can be misconstrued as just "bitch ambition." When all I really wanted, Martha, was just to do my job well, just do my job, that's all. But they wouldn't let me! I tried explaining all this to you in my letters but . . . They wouldn't leave me alone! So finally I left, wrote a letter, gave my resignation. Relinquished the precious turf. Packed up, fled, came here, hid, licked my wounds. Learned to live again, to breathe; to trust. *(Smiling.)* Here, where today my best friend, Martha, came and found me. I've missed you, I have. But I missed me too, Martha. *(Smiling.)* And here, well, I found me. Here, here, home.

(A beat, upbeat.) All right, enough about me, about all that. Tell me all about you, what you've been up to. I want to hear all of it, everything. My God, Martha, my God, it's so good to see you!

CHLOE
twenty-five and older
Comedic

After seeing Bob around town for years, Chloe finally has a date with him.

(Anxiously, nonstop, rambling.) It's all like predetermined, preordained, whatever you want to call it, Bob. Everyone knows it; ya learn it in Life 101. There are no accidents, no, none! Not even here, in small town U.S.A. We bump, melt, merge, whatever you want to call it, with people we are meant to meet, meant to meet! I believe that, I do. I mean think about it, just think about it, Bob; fact that you're here, I'm here, and we're both sitting in your car, front of my house; ready to go, night on the town, no accident, no-no-no. Preordained. And I want you to know, want you to know, Bob, I was thrilled when you called last week. Thought, oh my God, BOB, imagine, finally! After all these years! Not that I was sitting by the phone, no. I'm so busy these days at the library, nonstop, go-go-go; books back and forth; library lunacy. So you were really lucky to get me in, lucky I was even home. Luck, lucky, preordained. But it was certainly a surprise. I mean after all these years of seeing you at the supermarket, passing you on the street, seeing you drive by. Certainly a surprise. And now, here, the two of us, sitting in your car, waiting, waiting patiently, may I add, for you put the key in the ignition so we can go somewhere and . . . *(Looking at him.)* So why don't you start the car? Car can't start by itself. We can't go anywhere just sitting here.

(She turns to her door.) Why'd you open my door? . . . Bob, Bob, you don't want me to leave, do you? I can't go. No Bob, no, you don't understand, this is . . . This is a brand-new dress! This is our first . . . ! No, you don't understand. Bob, Bobby, Robert, this has all been — pre-ordained!

MARY
thirty and older
Dramatic

Here Mary talks gently and sincerely about her religious beliefs and her unusual job.

I believe in God, and I believe in the garbage man. One giveth and one taketh away. I suppose . . . suppose I see myself as somewhere in the middle, midway. I mean I've always had deep feelings about good and evil. Believed strongly that an eye for an eye is not just some tit for tat kind of thing. That in life there must be justice and a righteous retaliation. And the people around here who know me, know I believe this deeply. S'just the way I am, I guess, way I was brought up. Way I'm trying to bring my own kids up, with morals, ethics, convictions. So I wasn't shocked or anything when they made the offer. I mean who better if not me? *(A slight smile.)* Was a match made in heaven. Actually I was honored. I'm sure you've been hearing all about it, the press has been having a field day. I mean about me being the first woman to do it and all. Can't imagine why, the job doesn't require all that much. It's really no harder than turning on a light switch. Then there's the sound of course, the electric jolt. Room'll shake a bit. Sometimes you'll hear a gasp, one last scream. I like to think of that as their letting go of all evil within, their "redemption." Sometimes there's some smoke, some smell; and then it's all over. The air is clear, the slate is clean, the world's a better place. A silence, a peace . . . a moment I often savor. Then after, I'll help 'em with the cleanup, and then go on home to my kids. And I'll hug 'em, and kiss 'em, and sit and play with 'em, sometimes for hours.

MELANIE
any age
Comedic

Melanie joyfully recalls a great sale she caught.

I see that word, SALE, SALE, and I lose all sense of everything! My knees buckle, my hands start sweating. Everything in me says, DON'T, DON'T, but I do, enter, stand in the doorway. I know, I KNOW, I should walk away, but Bali Hai calls. And soon I fall down a wishing well into a land of magical markdowns. I'm drenched in a waterfall of "last day of sale" signs. I start to grab things, fight with other customers. "I had that first! Get your own!" It's survival of the fittest, and I'm a pro! Soon my pile becomes immense. I can't possibly carry all those clothes. I cry out! My guardian angel, a lovely salesgirl, floats down, touches my arm: "May I help you, miss?" She sees my distress. I immediately cry, "Yes, where's the fitting room?" And we start our trek to try-on heaven. But are stopped by the Nazilike fitting room gatekeeper who says, "Sorry, you can only take in eight items at a time." "Eight?!" I say, Why so few?!" Why not cut off an arm or leg? Sophie suffered nothing compared to this. Sophie's choice was small in comparison. How can I choose, which one first? The silk blouse, the Armani skirt? I agonize under her hateful eyes. She cruelly recounts each garment, then brands me with a bright-colored number eight.

Finally, the fitting room; four walls, a seat, a mirror. I get undressed, look at myself, feel unfinished; a naked caterpillar. Only new clothes can complete me. And as I try them on, I blossom into a bargain-basement butterfly. The bigger the markdown, the more I smile. And yes to this! And yes to that! My salesgirl dutifully waits outside my door. I rush to show her my choices. "Yes," she says. "That's lovely." And I know she means it.

As I pirouette for her as I used to do for Daddy. "Yes," she says, "that one too. That dress is you." And I agree, it is me — but at 50 percent off! Soon, many of these items will be taken home to my climate-controlled, walk-in closet, where they'll be hung on only wooden hangers, gently washed in Woolite, and dry cleaned only when needed.

Then that last journey to the cash register. I almost cry as I see each markdown fly by. The final item, my sale complete. Shopping bags in hand, I lovingly wave good bye to the entire sales staff of the store who are now standing in the doorway, saluting, bidding me a tear-filled goodbye. No please, please, don't cry. The Labor Day sales are only a few months away. Till then, kiss-kiss, adieu.

HENRIETTA
fifty-five and older
Serio-comedic

Henrietta talks about her perfect life with her husband, and her confusion about how it ended.

So on Friday, last Friday, he come in, just like always. Just like he'd done every day for over forty years. Kiss on the cheek, "Hi hon"; just like always. Had the dog with him, they'd been hunting. "Caught us a duck for dinner." Asked me to go out to the garden, to get us some vegetables. "Make us a nice stew," he said. So I walked, well, limped out to the garden, him and the dog following. Seemed odd since he'd always hated the garden. Anyway I'm bending down, my back busting from pain, getting us some nice carrots; when I heard him cock the gun. I looked up and he was pointing that gun right at me. I said, "Jack, what the hell you doing?" He was stone faced. "Jack, you crazy?! Jack, Jack, what?!" Then he shot. Shot me. Jack. Not once or twice, but six times. Last one hit me in the heart. Took him six to get me; he was never good with a gun. Bang-bang, I'm shot. Bang-bang, I fall. Bang-bang, I'm dead. Fell in the garden, crushed the cabbage. My stay on earth, ended. Why, Jack, why? We had a good life, over forty years together. Got three good kids, one even went to college. "Why, Jack, why?!"

He looked down at me, dead in the garden. I looked down at him standing there, alive. Then he sat down for a long time. Him and the dog sat quiet, all night long. In the morning, he got a shovel, buried me, disturbing the not-quite-ripened red tomatoes. No emotion, no, nothing. He's one of them quiet guys, y'know, can never tell what they're thinking. Then he went inside, called the sheriff, asked him if he would take care of the dog. Take care of the dog, why? Then he confessed what he'd done. Then he hung up, put the gun to his head.

Then bang-bang, Jack's dead. And in an instant, Jack joined me, here.

Well the farms up for sale, kids are selling it. And eventually everyone found out, why. Jack had gotten my medical report, it said cancer, said I had two months to live; said two months, tops, I was terminal. Well, my Jack does things in his own unique way.

The tomatoes in the garden have finally ripened.

Sometimes, sometimes it's the quiet ones who don't always hold your hand or say a helluva lot that'll love you forever. Forever, yeah, in their own quiet way.

Gwyneth
teens to early twenties
Comedic

Here Gwyneth, clinging to her chair, tries to figure out what she's doing alone on a theater stage.

(Confused and frightened.)
What,
what is this?
What's happening here?
                    Let me get my bearings.
                    Why am I feeling such fear?
                        My God,
                            what's going on here?!
        Why am I sitting on this stage?
        Why's he down there in that chair?

(Looking at him, still to herself.)

Look at you,
watching me.
        Didn't your mother ever tell you not to stare?

I'm sweating,
confused;
        but I've got an idea.
                    I think I know
                    WHY I'm up here.

I shouldn't be frightened.
                There's nothing at stake here.

Nothing at all,
except—
(A gasp.) my *career!*

(Trying to put it all together.)

My career?
Him staring?
Me sitting here in this chair.
I think there's something I'm supposed to do.
I'm supposed to be DOING something up here!

But what?
Tic-tock.
I think that there's words involved,
and memory ties into this whole thing.
Maybe I should ask—
"Excuse me,
was there something I was supposed to bring?"

He's getting impatient,
hates me,
I can see it in his eyes.
Maybe I should just go,
say my good-byes.

(She starts to get up, then quickly sits again.)

No!
I'm no coward.
I will not run,
no siree!

Whatever this nightmare is
        I won't let it take over me!
I will just sit here and . . .
        Wait;
            what's that?

(A slight smile, starting to get it.)

                It's—a memory.
                There's . . . there's words in the wings.
I'm starting to feel;

        My God, I'm starting to FEEL THINGS!
        And not just fear.

Oh my God,
        I know what's going on here!

(Finally realizing.)

The words . . . they're from a play.
        Something I worked on,
        rehearsed all day.
Memorized,
        made my own,
        It's a MONOLOGUE that I'm about to say!

        And this—
                is an audition.
                        And I am very well prepared.
And that sweet man down there
                is here to help me—with my career.

Oh he may not know it yet.
Probably hasn't the slightest idea.
But it's time to stand,

(She stands, smiles.)

    start my monologue,

(As she does.)

      and let go of this stupid chair.

BETTY

any age
Serio-comedic

Here Betty tells off her boyfriend.

(Very upset.) It's raining, I'm pissed, and you're depressed. Now if you want, if you really want to, Tom, we can continue sitting here in the dark. We can do that, yeah, sure, why not? We do it very well, have become "experts." Mean, why talk, right? Why bother talking when a look or grunt will do? Well, hey, how about this for an idea? How 'bout we try something unusual tonight; something we hardly ever do anymore? How about you and I try to *talk,* Tom! You know, like one word following another? Who knows, might be fun? We might even have a feeling fly in, some emotions might join the fray. Think you could handle it Tom; words, thoughts, *feelings?* Be like a goddamned communication orgy here. Tom, TOM, I'm talking to you! You used to talk, remember? I heard you loud and clear back in the bar that first time; couldn't shut you up. Talked a blue streak that night. Sweet things. Nice words. Compliments. *(Beat.)* Ya know, I feel sorry for you Tom, I do. You are a sad, pathetic person. You're dead inside, just don't know it. So sit there in the dark, dead. Sit there, I really don't care anymore. *(A beat.)* Look, I'm leaving. I'm going now. I'm tired of talking. Tired of wondering if you're even listening; if you're awake! HEY ARE YOU AWAKE, TOM?! . . . I'm going. Please, don't get up, I can find my way in the dark, have been doing it . . . 'Sides why

ruin a good Saturday night by turning on the light, right? I'll use my key, let myself out, just like always. *(A beat, softer.)* Look, I'll call ya, okay? I'll call ya, next Saturday, all right? Same time, seven? . . . Call ya Tom, I'll call, ya.

YVONNE
any age
Serio-comedic

Yvonne lovingly talks about her baby boy.

(Smiling.) He was a bouncing baby boy; with a round little face. And when I'd diaper him, I'd always say *(Playful baby talk.)*, "Who's Mommy's little boy?" And he'd giggle, get so excited, that sometimes he'd pee, straight up, like a little yellow geyser. And I'd say *(Playfully.)*, "Who's peeing on his Mommy?" And he'd giggle again. Then I'd clean him up, and kiss him. And oh, oh how he loved to be powdered! *(Blushing.)* It, well, "excited" him. So I'd say, *(Playfully.)*, "Who's got a little hard-on here?" And he'd giggle again. Then I'd diaper him, lift him up, walk with him around the room. Then I'd take him back to my bedroom, put him on the bed, and say "Who's Mommy's little boy?" Then I'd lie down next to him, and just look at him. And sometimes he'd look up at me, and we'd stare at each other, till his eyes would slowly start to close. And then he'd fall asleep. And I'd lay there on the bed next to him, watching him sleep; sometimes, sometimes for hours.

LINDA-ANNE
any age
Dramatic

Linda-Anne, who grew up in a small town, recalls the last day she saw her father.

(A painful memory.) I was in my room playing with my dolls. Daddy came in, seemed upset. He grabbed my arm, yelled, "Come with me!"

Never seen him so angry. His face was beet red, veins in his neck were bulging. I was young, but I knew this was bad. Daddy dragged me like a rag doll. Thought he'd rip my arm right off.

"What I do? What I do, Daddy?"

The rooms were spinning by; the walls and windows blurring. "Where's Momma? I want Mommy!" He pulled me right outta the house. Was hot outside, burning hot that day. Daddy threw me in the car. I smelled liquor on his breath. But liquor usually made him laugh. Then Daddy locked me in the car, went back in the house.

I heard screamin', hollerin'. Then I saw Momma come runnin' out on the porch. She was bleedin' bad. I screamed to her. The heat in the car was burnin', I couldn't breathe. Daddy was hittin' her, hard, again and again. Never seen him so mad. Momma was bleeding from everywhere. I screamed, but she couldn't hear me. I tried opening the car doors, but they were locked. Daddy dragged Momma back in the house. Then there was this loud sound. It was a gunshot. Was the loudest noise I ever heard. Car was burnin' hot. Sleep. Sleepy. Humpty-Dumpty had a great fall. Humpty-Dumpty fell off the wall.

(A beat.) Neighbors broke the car windows. Someone yelled, "She's still alive!" Ambulance. Doctors. Bright lights. And all the king's horses, and all the king's men, couldn't put Humpty together again.

When I woke up, Momma was there with Aunt Grace.

"How you feelin', child?"

She fixed my hair, smiled. Her eyes were swollen bad, her face was all cut up.

"Where's Daddy?"

Momma looked over at Aunt Grace, Aunt Grace just looked away. Then Momma held me, tightest hug ever. And I dozed off in her arms.

"And all the king's horses, and all the king's men, couldn't put Humpty back together again."

HARRIET
any age
Comedic

Harriet anxiously describes why she has run out of the bedroom of a man she just met at a bar.

I'm so sorry, so . . . ! Something just happened! Something happened in there. I don't . . . I needed to come out here; catch my breath. I'm so, so sorry. Suddenly I couldn't breathe, isn't that crazy? Inside, in the dark, in the bed, I got so scared all of a sudden, suddenly. I mean isn't that nuts, to be frightened like that of the dark? I don't know what happened. I mean everything was wonderful. Here we were having a great time, and I ruin it, kill the mood, jump out of bed, run out here screaming like a crazy woman. You must be thinking, Jesus H. Christ, I've got a koo-koo bird here. Who let this loony tune loose? Must be thinking, shit, I should have left this one at the bar. This has never happened, Nate, never, no! And believe me I go home with guys all the time, all-the-time! I mean come Friday night I get through work, go the bar, have a drink, meet and greet, find a guy, let off steam; no big deal. Harmless, playful, fun. So what just happened in there must have been some sort of a momentary "flip out." But I'm fine now, Nate; I've flipped back in. The bogeyman's buried, my breath is back. Even my shaking's stopped, see? I'm fine, fine, really.

(A breath, smiling, cheerful.) So, all that being said, and what a mouthful it was, what do you say we go back in, get under the covers, and pick up where we left off? You still "up" for it; wanna take another spin around the dance floor? Huh Nate, what do you say?

THELMA
fifty and over
Dramatic

Thelma recalls her loving relationship with her grandson.

I hated going there, that house, them hollering all the time! The two of them, the tension, you could cut it with a . . .! Then one day he left, left my daughter, without a pot to piss in. Can you imagine? A woman with a kid, stranded. So who else she got turn to, a stranger on the street? No, me, her mother. Like I didn't have enough to do, right? Had my own problems back then, a husband not much better than hers. And to boot, I had a business, my bar to run. My plate was full, my cup. . . . I mean who the hell had time to take care of a kid?! But she had to work, support herself. And he was my grandson. What could I do, deny her? She's my daughter, family. So finally I said okay, I'll help you with him. So I'd go there every morning, give him his breakfast, bring him to the bar, put him in a booth, give him his coloring book, and let him play. He was a good kid, quiet. Could entertain himself, easy to take care of. He'd just sit there all day, coloring away. Long as he had them crayons and that coloring book, the world was a perfect place. And "Grandma, I love you," he'd say. A hug, a kiss. And I'd feed him his lunch, he'd smile, then go back to his book, coloring away, losing himself in them pictures. He was just a sweet, happy-go-lucky kid, who, thank God, thank God, didn't know from nothing.

ANGELA
adult
Comedic

Angela gives a strong warning to a woman whose friend has tried to upset her marriage.

I don't need your friend Carmen tellin' me nothing 'bout Sal. See, I'm not her father confessor, so Carmen can keep her secrets to herself. Mean when it comes to Sal, no one needs to tell me nothin'. Since our first date at that diner in Patterson, Sal has held little or no mystery to me. Know the man like the back of my hand. So when *Carmen*, little bitch *Carmen* comes waltzin' in here to unload her secrets, confess her sins with him to me, well, I let her know it was of no interest to me. But despite my repeated warnings, she chose to continue, and with a fervor! So finally, ladylike, I asked her to please cease and desist. But Carmen-would-not-stop! So I let the back of my hand *speak* to the front of her face. And after several visits of my clenched fist, well, Carmen can now skip her next doctor's visit for collagen for her lips.

Look, I know she's your friend, so I assume that you'd warn her about strolling into a lion's den looking for some sort of sympathy. I mean who she does, or what she does, is of no goddamned interest to me. But you and I both know that you don't come round for little social visits when you're planning on putting arsenic in the wife's tea.

Look, I gotta go, Sal's waitin' for his supper. I really meant your friend no harm, really. I mean if I see her on the street, I might even say hi. But I think it's definitely in her best interest that you educate her about the ins and outs of our little social scene out here. 'Cause I'll tell ya, the wife of the next husband she sleeps with, may be inclined to use more than just a fist.

ANNIE-MAY
late teens to early twenties
Serio-comedic

Annie-May recalls a terrifying date.

I showed up at the diner over a half hour early. I was so nervous. Well you know, you saw, I was a wreck. Got a booth in the back. Margo came over, asked me what I wanted. Ordered some coffee. Caffeine, just what I needed, right? Margo asked if I was all right. I said "Sure, have a date, little nervous."

"Date?" she said. "Well, la-de-da." She's was bein' so smug, wanted to smack her. Hate her sometimes, don't you? Didn't dare tell her it was someone I met on the internet. She told me I looked nice. Asked if my dress was new.

"Just bought it, Laytons."

"Stylish," she said. "Pretty."

"Margo," I said, "Don't you have any other customers?"

"Sorry," she said, "Have a nice date."

She left, and there I was alone with my nerves. Kept lookin' out the window, waitin'. Seemed like hours.

Then I heard a car pull into the parking lot. Car door opened, than shut. I couldn't breathe, Linda, I could not breathe! Door to the diner opened. It was him, I just knew it! I didn't dare turn around. Wanted it to be like a movie moment; ya know, Julia Roberts meets Richard Gere. Then he touched me, Linda, my right shoulder. I slowly turned, my smile, prepared and ready. My well-rehearsed, "Why Bob, how nice to finally meet you." But when I looked up, there was this *much older* man! He said, "You Annie-

May"? I said, "Yes," but I wanted to say, "Who are you? Where's Bob; you his father?"

He sat down next to me. I couldn't move, couldn't talk. He was as old as my father! Stringy white hair, fat, ugly, with thick, dark glasses. He lied, Linda! That picture he sent musta been taken a hundred years ago. He had yellow stained teeth, looked like fangs. And his dirty fingers looked like claws. He was old, I was scared!

"Wanna go for a ride?" he said.

His breath stunk, halitosis.

"Ride? Car? You?"

Margo came over, smiled, said, "They finally fixed the toilet. Remember, you asked me to tell you when they fixed it?"

I caught her cue, turned to Bob, said "Be right back." Went with Margo to the kitchen. She started laughin', said "Is Grandpa your date?" She opened the back door, let me out. I ran home fast as I could. My new dress was a mess. Collapsed on my bed, cried hysterical. Then I went to my computer, sent Bob a "So long, you're a big liar!" e-mail.

He was the date from hell. I'm tellin' ya, Linda, my dream date was a real nightmare.

KAREN

any age
Dramatic

Karen recalls a terrifying experience in a plane.

(Intensely.) My fingers dig into his hand, deeper, deeper! Bells going off; gasps, cries! People calling out, "Mama!" Jesus!" The overhead cabinets pouring out. This is not a dream or drill; there's no doubt we're going down. In an instant the shift becomes sharper! The plane is pointing almost straight down. Things start falling, trays, cushions! Clouds, which only a few seconds ago seemed like cotton balls, rush by my window like white razors cutting the night. Dishes crash, oxygen masks dangle in the dark.

Wasn't it just a moment ago I said, "Would you please pass the coffee." He smiled, too friendly, I looked away. My obvious but polite message, "Forget it, mister, I'm married." Everything was quiet, calm. But now, chaos, as we're surrounded by a chorus of people's screams.

"Prepare for impact! Prepare for impact!" We suddenly cling close to each other. Through the window on the other side, I see the ocean coming closer, closer!

(A change, gently.) But then . . . suddenly everything softens. Gentle, slow. The panic becomes serene. The passengers' screams now seem like little children, laughing. Then a loving voice somewhere in the distance calls, "Come on home." As I suddenly soften in his arms, and he holds me, and I realize there's nothing to be afraid of, no. I'm just going home, home with him. Sister-brother, mother-father; instant family. As we cling tightly, tenderly, like lovers. Till soon all sounds cease. Till soon — all time stops. And soon we're forced to finally let go.

KIT
a senior citizen
Serio-dramatic

Here Kit, a senior citizen, offers an explanation to the store manager at a fine jewelry store.

Why? Because I got tired of rice pudding and seeing people staring into space in Siberia. Making new friends and then seeing them slowly slip into dementia. Going south without saying "good-bye, Kit, nice knowing ya." Too much loss makes you lonely, mister.

My sweet son and his oh-so-good intentions. A whisk of the broom, magic carpet ride, my house was gone, and so was my independence. Then his sad Sunday visits, his guilt- filled phone calls. "You're forgiven son, just pray your kids don't do this to you." Well, I assume he meant well.

So finally, Friday, after giving it less than an ounce of thought, I just left. No good-byes, no thank yous, no need. Left a don't-worry-about-me note, a plate of stewed prunes, and an uneaten baked apple. Felt like a young girl, night on the town, a new adventure. I don't know about you, mister, but me, without my freedom, I cannot breathe, I lose my breath. And since the first day I moved into that place, my breath became "constipated." But these last few days, since I've been sprung, I have been on a BREATH-ING SPREE! My lungs have reopened, and I have enjoyed every moment, every morsel of life! Grabbed onto anything that wasn't old or decaying. And well, perhaps in all that grabbing and taking, I took in more than I should. Perhaps I was caught up in the rush of my release. And maybe that's why I took that gold watch and the jewelry; the risk, the danger! I'm not denying it, no, I did it, guilty as charged! You can have it all back, every piece. But please, don't call them, tell them I'm here. Send me to jail, I don't care. Prison might be fun, all those young, *alive* criminals. Can only be better than that wasteland of wheelchairs, dying and dementia. Now that I have my breath back, my second wind, please, mister, don't send me back to — Siberia.

BERNICE WEINSTEIN
thirty and older
Comedic

Bernice lambastes her husband about not being able to find ketchup.

(An angry tirade.) Don't! Don't tell me what I just said, Sid! Know exactly what I . . . ! You asked me where the ketchup was; the ketchup! And I clearly said, "The ketchup's in the kitchen on the counter." Clear, simple English. Never said fridge, NOT FRIDGE, NO! Ketchup — kitchen — counter! If you keep the ketchup in a fridge, it sometimes freezes, everyone knows that, idiot. So I'm sittin', wondering where the hell's Sid? How long can it take to walk to a kitchen? My french fries are freezing, my chicken's turning green. So now I come in here and see this? In my just-cleaned kitchen, on my just-waxed floor? What'cha do, imbecile, empty out the whole refrigerator?! Look at this place, it's a mess! Now get up off the floor and put it all back. All you had to do is look over there. See? S'just like I said, The KETCHUP'S IN THE KITCHEN ON THE COUNTER! The counter, by the cupboard over there! You're a moron; I'm sorry I ever married you. Biggest mistake of my life. But this is it, it's over, this is the last straw! I'm through with you, understand?! We are done, I-want-a-DIVORCE! I'm tired of being married to an alcoholic, out-of-work idiot. Consider your meal ticket torn! First thing tomorrow, I'm filing for divorce. Now put all that stuff back! Did you hear . . . ?! Oh I see, NOW you're going to get the ketchup from the counter. Now? Hey what are you doing, why are you opening that drawer?

I said the counter! Sid, I'm talking to you! Sid . . . Sid put the knife back in the drawer. That's not funny, it's sharp, you'll cut yourself. Why are you laugh . . . ? *(Backing away.)* Sid, look, I was just kidding! No divorce, okay? I promise, no divorce! *(Frightened, backing away, a forced smile.)* Sid, what are you doing? Sid, you just keep away! Keep away, understand?! *(Becoming terrified.)* KEEP . . . ! STOP . . . ! *(Screaming.)* SID!

Tina
adult
Comedic

Here Tina, a very wealthy woman, talks seductively to one of her dinner guests.

(Playful, soft, and seductive.)
Make your move.
Don't be shy.
Come on over here.

(Smiling.)
It's okay,
     my husband's down in the den,
                    downstairs.
So there's absolutely nothing to fear.
He's busy doing business with the boys.
         So why are you standing way over there?

(A beat.)
Am I being too forward?
Suddenly you seem so shy.
Earlier I thought I saw a certain something in your eye.
Something that said you wanted to play.
I mean from the minute you arrived,
when I opened the door;
        your eyes, my dear —
           were giving it away.
And all through dinner,
I noticed your little stares.

That's why I asked you to join me here,
                              upstairs.
If I'm wrong,
        my apologies,
              forgive me,
                    my dear.

I certainly didn't mean to offend.
I was just hoping
              that we could become good friends.
Just two girls,
        some fun,
              without any old men.

But if you want to leave
              I'll get out of your way.

(She moves away.)
I certainly don't want to be with anyone
              who doesn't want to stay.

(A beat.)
You've put your drink down.
              And you're smiling.
                    So what does that say?
Tell me if I'm wrong —

(Smiling.)
                    but it certainly seems like now you
want to stay.

(Putting her drink down.)
Well, I'll put my drink down too.

See, just like you.
And stand here,
            and wait
                        for you to make your move;
                        and show me
                        exactly what you'd
                        like — to do.

SADIE

fifty and older
Dramatic

Sadie fondly remembers her mother.

My mother was a strong, good woman. Knew what she wanted, very determined. Born in a small town in Russia, God, probably isn't even there anymore. S'where she met my father, they fell in love, got married, came here to America. My father was a small, frail man. Drove his horse and cart through the streets selling ice. Long days, hard work, took its toll. We were poor but we got by. And after Daddy died, Momma did cleaning, washing, whatever. Raised me and my sisters best she could. Was tough on her, c'mon, three daughters, woman alone back then. But she did the best she could! But she was tough, I'll tell ya. You broke the rules in our house, you paid for it dearly. Disobey her, you got a beating but good. Say a dirty word, you got your mouth washed out with soap. And if you ever, God forbid, gave her lip, you got the back of a belt! We'd all run and hide in corners, could get very scary, yeah. But we always knew momma was doing it for our own good. That she loved us, just didn't have time for any kutchy-koo. Wasn't her nature, no. But we all knew, we knew she loved us. And for us, well, that was enough.

GLORIA
any age
Dramatic

Gloria furiously confronts her husband after a painful discovery.

Yeah, I'd like it to be nice, yeah sure! Kiss on the cheek, ten years of marriage, so long, see ya, bye bye. I'd like that, Larry, yeah, sure! But are you NUTS?! It can NEVER be nice now, never! Throw any thoughts of NICE out the window! NICE is no longer an option!

But for now, Larry, there's Gabe. He has no idea what Daddy's been doing. Has no idea what kind of pervert his papa is. Gabe's clueless, like Mommy WAS! Mommy, who was always too busy just being "Mommy."

"Take Gabe to school, dear."

"Sure"

"Take Gabe to the game, hon."

"Of course."

I wondered why you couldn't come with us today. Why you always seem to be too busy. Never dawned on me . . . ! Then to walk in here, and see you . . . HERE, IN OUR HOUSE. IN OUR BED — YOU SON OF A BITCH!

You know, you think you know someone, love them, trust them. Think you know them inside out. And then . . . And with a child, a CHILD, IN OUR BED! Don't you ever come near me or your son again, or I swear, I'll have you arrested on the spot. I'm going to go burn those sheets in the backyard. And when I come back you better be gone. 'Cause if you're not, I swear to Christ, I will sit your son down, and as young as he is, tell him exactly what his daddy's been doing. *(Staring at him.)* Now get out of my sight. Far as I'm concerned, Larry, you never existed. Now that's my version of NICE.

Cynthia
forties and older
serio-comedic

Here Cynthia talks about how she got by being a single mother during rough times.

(*A small tirade.*) I provided for him, Harold, made sure he never went without! That he was nicely dressed, looked like something! I was home here with him every night, while Sam, Sam, that son of bitch, was out screwing anything, everything! Oh I knew, c'mon, everyone, the whole neighborhood knew. Casanova; couldn't keep it in his pants. Big mistake my marrying that man. My mother had to help me out here with Harold. Couldn't do it alone, raise a son by myself. And my mother, she had a business to run, didn't have time to take care of kids. But she did, baby-sat, whatever. We-did-the-best-we-could! Times were different back then; men could get away with . . . And Sam's alimony checks? Ha, I'm still waiting, over twenty years! If I depended on those checks, Harold and I would've have been living out on the streets under cardboard boxes in the rain. So I got a job, part-time, paid the bills. We got by, barely, but we got by. Sam was a waste, a dent in my life! I'm glad he's dead! Did his damage, now he's gone. Closed chapter, ancient history, turn the page. You move on, that's all. Bring up your kid the best you can. You spit on any regrets and learn from your mistakes. You-just-move-on!

STEPHANIE
adult
Dramatic

Here, Stephanie sits in a bar, having had a few drinks, while looking out the window at people going by.

I sit and drink, and watch and wonder, where's everybody going? Sit in my seat here at the bar and think, "What's the rush?" I want to say, "Slow down, don't worry, he'll be there." He'll be on the couch, watching TV, just like, just like always. And he'll kiss you hello and you'll smile, sit next to him and tell him all about your day. And he'll half listen, while watching the six o'clock news. But then he'll look at you, smile that smile, and you'll just melt, cuddle up close, not say a word. No need, no. Be just the two of you silently watching the six o'clock news; just like, just like always.

(Building in intensity.) So where are you people all rushing?! It's only the middle of the afternoon! Are you worried he might not be there? That maybe he left? He'd never do that, no! Because then you'd always wonder why, what went wrong, where'd he go? And then you'd start to run, run fast! Anywhere, anywhere, so you won't have to be home, alone. Anywhere, so you won't have to watch the six o'clock news by yourself. But don't worry, stop running, that could never NEVER happen to you — no!

(A beat, softer.) So come inside, have a drink, maybe, maybe have a few. Look out the window, watch the people rush by. Listen to the music. Come . . . sit . . . and watch.

SYBIL
forty and older
Dramatic

Sybil tells her son how unhappy her married life was with his father.

Everytime I turned around, there he was, like a shadow! At first it felt . . . was kind of cute; y'know, all that attention. But it never let up. Your father, he was like obsessed! When we got back from our honeymoon, he was always around, on top of me. He'd follow me from room to room. Even to the store — he was like a stalker! That's not love, no! When a person's on top of you like that, always touching, and wanting — no DEMANDING — sex. Times were different back then, a women had to . . . So I'd lie there, let him, just let him. Go off in my head somewhere. Pretend. Escape. Wait for it to be over, then turn around, make like I was asleep.

But eventually, it got to the point where he . . . he repulsed me, your father. His . . . everything! The sight of him, his body, breath, even knowing he was in the house. That's when the arguments began. The fights over anything, everything. Then you were born. And I thought, well hoped . . . But the fights only got worse. Think he was jealous of you. I never felt as lonely, as alone, in my whole life, as when I lived with that man. And I'm sorry to say it, but I was glad the day he died.

MARCIA
any age
Serio-comedic

Marcia recalls a terrifying health scare.

"Mela — what??! Mela—what?!"

"Melanoma," he said.

"What?!"

"Skin cancer."

"No, it's just a freckle!

"'Fraid not," he said. But we can take care of it, we caught it early. Simple surgery, right here in my office, now. Then we'll send it off, see what they say."

I sat there, shocked. Cancer, a word I've heard since I was a kid. "Melanoma," it sounded like a mystical island. Somewhere where you drink piña coladas under a tropical sun, as it seduces you, whispers, "It's okay, relax, you're safe. "But there in the doctor's office, I felt anything but.

And so it came to pass that my innocent freckle was excavated, taken somewhere to be determined how serious it was. It would lie in a lab among countless other recently plucked freckles, all of whom had stories to tell of sun burned days and Bain de Soleil.

Sleepless nights, endless worry, vacation regrets. Early one morning I went to the bathroom, poured out every bottle of tanning oil, then went to the window, looked up at the sun, and cried, "You did this, you bastard! Then I lifted my fist to the sky and said, "As the lord is my witness, I'll never get tan again!"

When I went back to the doctor, he told me we'd gotten it all. The tests said I was A-okay, but he insisted I stay out of the sun from now on. I smiled, told him my next vacation would be in Alaska, in the dark of winter. The doctor laughed, then left. I stood in his office, grateful. While walking home I noticed what a beautiful day it was. The sun was bright, warm, inviting. I quickly bought an umbrella, opened it, and went merrily on my way.

Anita

a young mom
Dramatic

Anita talks about a terrifying experience she recently went through with her baby boy.

We'd just finished dinner, Dan was putting the dishes away. I told him I'd go upstairs, check on Charlie, was time for his feeding. I went up to our room, turned the light on, he was quiet, unusual. Usually when I turned the light on . . . I went to his crib, bent down, and I knew, knew right away. He wasn't moving, his eyes were closed. He wasn't breathing! I called his name, nothing. Moved him, shook him, then screamed to Dan. Could hear Dan running from downstairs! At that moment I believe I just went insane. Dan came running into the room. I screamed, "HE'S NOT BREATHING!!" Dan went to the crib, looked down, picked him up, placed Charlie on the floor. Dan started breathing into his mouth, deep, deep breaths. "Dan don't let him die!" The room started spinning. Dan kept taking deep, full breaths. And all I could think, all that went through my mind was "No, no, not our baby!" I stood next to Dan, looking down; was like watching him from a million miles away. Dan was breathing, moving, slow motion. Someone was screaming, perhaps it was me. Then finally, from somewhere in the distance I heard a voice. It was Dan's voice. It was Dan saying . . . Dan said . . . "HE'S BREATHING! Call 9-1-1!" Charlie was choking, coughing. Charlie was BREATHING! Dan was smiling, said "It's okay, honey, call 9-1-1. Charlie was crying. Dan was crying. I quickly got the phone, called, they came.

(A beat.) Just a freak thing, the doctor said. Wasn't quite sure why it happened. But the miracle, he said, was that I went to his room when I did. Another few minutes . . . So Charlie's fine. Every day something new. Every day, a new discovery. He said his first word yesterday, it was "Mommy." He said, "Mommy." Well, that's what I think he said. *(Smiling.)* But he might have just said, "Mumum" or something. Anyway, Charlie's fine. . . . Charlie's great. . . . Charlie's okay.

VENETIA
thirty and older
Dramatic

After tolerating her husband's constant put-downs, she finally tells him off.

Your words feel like a fork, and you keep jabbing at me. What's the game tonight, to destroy or just maim me? Look, I'm on to you; I-am-on-to-you! You tell our friends how much you love me. Tell my mother how happy we are. Nice act, very convincing. But then every night, here, alone, the two of us, the little jabs you claim are jokes are no longer funny. And your constant commenting about how thin those fashion models are, and wouldn't it be great if I could lose some weight, has become more than annoying. I feel fine the way I am. I like my body EXACTLY the way it is. When's the last time you looked in a mirror, Ted? That tube around your waist, that's called a belly! Too many jelly donuts, Ted, too many daiquiris before dinner. So I've had it with your jokes, your put-downs. This isn't what I signed on for. We were in love once, remember? We treated each other with kindness and respect. And if we can't get back to that, the way it was, I'm out of here! I won't put up with it any longer. So what I'm saying, Ted is, if you want a punching bag, go out and buy one!

INA

adult

Dramatic

Here Ina confronts her former lover at an intervention.

(Powerfully.) Don't you get it, WE HAD TO! Was the only way to get you here. Look, I know you hate me right now, wanna kill me. Well let me tell you somethin', boyo, there have been times in the last few years, that I SWEAR, if I'd had a knife, I'd have slit your goddamned throat. Just look at you, what you've become! Look at yourself! I remember who you once were. And those memories still live inside of me, sealed. So sit there and hate me, hate all of us here, I really don't care. All I know is that this is the end of it, it's over tonight. And if you decide to keep using, I'll make you a deal, I'll become your new dealer. And I'll give what you've been looking for since that first pill. The perfect drug, the final ride: death, the ultimate high. If after all this you keep using, I'll kill you myself, I swear I will. For love, baby, for nothing — for old time's sake.

NETTI

adult
Dramatic

Netti has an emotional reunion with her sister.

(Very excited.) I can't believe it, pinch me, give me a hug! Can't believe this is happening! Pinch me, pinch me! So many years, so many dreams. But I knew it, I did, Something inside just knew! But they kept saying no, telling me I was wrong. But I knew that somewhere in this world was you. Somewhere was Sarah, my big sister. And look at you, so beautiful, such a beautiful woman.

(Suddenly rambling.) Let me tell you about me. I have a daughter, I do. What am I saying? I have two kids, two; Stephen and Stephanie, beautiful, both of 'em. Wait'll you see. My husband's name is Sandy, he's an accountant. You'll like him, very nice, funny guy. We live near Miami Beach, well actually Boca. And we both . . . *(Suddenly stopping herself.)* What am I doing here? What am I going on about? Why am I telling you all this now? We got the rest of our lives to talk.

(A beat, a breath.) I can't believe that this is real. Come here and pinch me, hug me. Tell me this isn't a dream. Come give me a kiss. C'mon, don't be so shy. Why are you still standing way over there? . . . Hey, where you going? Where are you going?! No, stop, don't fly away. Come back down here! Where are you going? This isn't a dream, not again! Sarah, come here, hold me. *(She pinches herself.)* Pinch me, pinch me!! *(Pinching herself harder, looking up.)* Don't let this be a dream. No, no, no!

GRACE
twenties to thirties
Comedic

Grace, a neurotic lady, declares her independence.

(A tirade.) Needy?! No, not at all. I am not needy! I'm not needy, no! And I know, I know what you're thinking. You're thinking she's saying she's not needy, which really means she is. Well I'm not; that thought won't work, I'm on to you. I happen to feel fabulous today, so ha, ha! And just because I asked you to do me a favor this one time is no reason to call me names. You are small, you know that, very, very small. And trying to belittle me, bring me down to your size, will no longer work. Not here, not now, not anymore. It's independence day, ha! And I'm a queen on a throne. And if calling me names like "needy" is what it takes to make you feel like a man, well I feel sorry for you; I do. So you can just leave, get out of here! GO, did you hear me! The queen has spoken. Just because I asked you this one time to stay home from school and watch TV with me, doesn't make me needy—no! Why are you still standing there? Go get your lunch from the fridge and leave. And take all your toys with you. Hurry up, before you miss your bus. I can watch TV all alone. Mommy doesn't need you, no. Mommy is a queen on a throne. Mommy is NOT needy, no!

ELLEN

any age
Serio-comedic

Here Ellen tells her fiancé about a car accident she once had.

It was an accident. The road was wet and I was tired. So maybe, maybe I don't know, maybe I was driving too fast. I just remember wanting to get home, get to bed. I made this turn at the top of a hill. And there was this curve, and next thing I knew, there was this old man, right in front of my car. I slammed on the brakes! But there was this sound, like a thump. Next thing I knew he was all over my windshield. Car kept swerving, round and round! I was trying to steer while looking right at his face, blood, bleeding down my windshield! Spinning, swerving, until finally the car stopped; it just stopped! And it was quiet, just the rain. I sat there, looking right at him, the man on my windshield. His face this close to mine, his eyes wide open. And all I could think was "Oh God, please don't be dead." Then I got out, went to the windshield, touched him, moved him; nothing. There was no doubt, he was dead. He must have been about eighty, gray hair, raincoat, wedding ring . . . wedding ring. I stood there in the rain, saying "I'm so sorry, so sorry." Then I looked around to see if anyone saw. No one. Then I . . . I pushed him off the hood; he fell down to the ground. Then with all my strength I rolled him over to the edge, by the cliff. And with one last shove I pushed him over. And he rolled down for what seemed like forever, through bushes and rocks. I waited until finally he stopped. Then I looked around again, then quickly got back in the car, drove home, and cried. My God, I must have cried that whole night. . . . They found his body about a month later. No one ever knew who did it. It's remained my secret, until now.

(A beat, then smiling.) So that's it, the one thing I've never told anyone. You're the first, honey. Pretty amazing, huh? Why are you looking at me like that? C'mon, it's your turn now. C'mon, honey, tell me your big secret!

MYRIAM
twenties to forties
Dramatic

After making love with Johnny, a guy she knows from a bar, Myriam tells him why he has to leave.

I believe in love, that's why I want you to leave. Just get dressed, Johnny, please. *(He doesn't.)* . . . Baby, c'mon, tonight was fun. We finally did what we've been wanting to since that first night at Flannigans. Since that first smile, that first wink, that first drink. We both knew tonight was coming; well it came. And now it's over, and it's time to go. C'mon, Johnny, please. *(He doesn't.)* Johnny, Johnny, don't do this, c'mon. We had so much fun, why ruin it? I'm tired, and tomorrow's a work day. Johnny, don't look at me that way. Let's just end this now, nice. Leave, and I'll watch you from my window. I'll stand there like some love-struck Doris Day. Then I'll go to sleep and dream only about you, baby. See, I do believe in love. But only the magical, uncomplicated, one-night-at-a-time type. Where everything's perfect, and it ends one minute before midnight. Where the dream isn't too real, and the memory is forever. I believe in love more than you can imagine. But now the glass slipper's gone, the coach is about to turn into a pumpkin. I'll see you next Friday — at Flannigans. And I'll wink and you'll smile, and we'll both know how wonderful tonight was; and it was. So for love, Johnny, for dreams, for now . . . please, leave.

Men's Monologues

HERM

any age
Dramatic

Herm passionately talks about his deep love for Julia.

(Smiling.) I bring her breakfast in bed, every Sunday. Bananas on granola, her favorite. Tell her household help to take the day off. S'just me and Julia, alone. We'll lie out in the sun, talk, and she'll tell me all kinds of things; Julia tells me everything. Then a little later, we'll make love, then have lunch. Then lie out in the sun and maybe have a margarita; just the way Julia likes it, not too much salt.

(Beat.) She's really not who you think she is. With me she's different. She's not some big movie star, she's just my Julia. All that put-on confidence, that smiley veneer, not with me, no. When we're alone, Julia is just very, very scared. So I take care of her, comfort her, let her know it's all going to be okay. *(Smiling.)* I bring her breakfast in bed, serve her sliced banana on granola. *(A slow change.)* I do everything to keep all evil away. And evil surrounds her, it does. It flies around her house in swarms; dark yellow clouds of danger. It's everywhere, she knows it, and it frightens her. Sometimes Julia becomes terrified. But she knows that if anyone, I mean ANYONE tries to hurt her, I will kill them; they will be *destroyed!* And as for those security guards, c'mon, everyone knows what a goddamned joke they are. *(Leaning in.)* All they want, all they really want to do is fuck her, rape her! She's a big movie star, and everyone, everyone wants a piece, a slice, a chunk! They all just want to tear into her, chew her up in

bite-size pieces. Then gnaw on her thin body, then lick her bones. Someone has to protect her!

So I was there today to help, to help Julia. She called and I came, and she let me in. Hey, I told you guys, I'm the man who BRINGS HER GRANOLA FOR BREAKFAST, ME! AND I CAREFULLY CHOP THAT BANANNA WITH A KNIFE, PIECE BY PIECE; *VERY, VERY, VERY SLOWLY!*

(Softly.) So if you'll just call her, you'll see. You'll see, she'll say *(Softer.)*, "Herm, where are you? Help me, I'm scared. The dark yellow clouds are everywhere; they frightened me. Please Herm, hurry, come soon. Help me Herm, I'm very . . . very . . . scared."

LEN

adult
Comedic

Here Len joyfully recalls his first one.

She was my first. What can I say? I was a kid. Small town, nothing else to think about, nothing to do. And all I knew, all I knew was I wanted her, had to have her. Well you're a guy, you know how it is.

First time I saw her, I'll never forget. I was with some friends. We were walking downtown, and there she was. I mean there — she — was! And all of us, jaws dropped, the whole thing. A sacred moment, no one said a word. And I made up my mind right then and there, that someday she'd be mine. I mean who the hell was I? Just some piss-poor kid, but that didn't stop me. See sometimes, sometimes, son, you have to have a dream, become obsessed. It instills determination, then perseverance kicks in. Know what I mean? So I busted my butt, took any job I could, saved, earned. I was going to make her mine!

(A smiling wink.) Never forget the first time I was inside of her, wow! Wow-wow-wow! Let me tell you, let me tell you, son, being *inside* that first time is something else. Her smell, way she felt. Someday you'll see what I mean. There's nothing like it. Makes you feel like a man, knowing she's all yours. That she'll do whatever you want. And she had a body on her that — that would not quit. Think I still have some pictures of her upstairs in the attic. Maybe we'll go up later and I'll show 'em to you. Just don't tell your mother. Always thought she was a little jealous. Women, huh, go figure.

(A beat.) All right, so what's it gonna be? You gonna get a job, or depend on me for the bucks? It's your call, buddy. Like I said, if you really want something, you've gotta work for it, earn it. It'll mean that much more. I mean we're talking about your first car here, and that's something very special. Trust me, kid, when it comes to cars, when it comes to a man's car, you never forget your first.

Ronald

adult

Serio-dramatic

Ronald talks about his recent prison experience.

(Smiling, but with an edge.) Bitter? No. Resentful? Why should I be? I'm free. She just made a mistake, that girl, thought I was someone else. You've got to forgive and forget, and I do and I did. I simply wasn't who she thought I was; mistakes happen. And unfortunately, sometimes the wrong folks get put away. Happens; happens. And sometimes it takes twenty-two years for the truth to finally be revealed. Twenty-two years till some overworked legal-aid lawyer can finally prove, beyond a shadow of a goddamned doubt, that I really didn't do it! But hey, there was no DNA back then, so it was really no one's "fault." 'Sides, that girl, she swore on a bible that I raped her. She was sure and she swore. But I'm certain she's sorry now. Folks just look like other folks, I guess. Mistakes happen.

And if nothing else, hey, I made a whole new bunch of friends in there. Guys I got to know very, very, well. Guys who taught me all kinds of things, from top to bottom. Was a real eye-opener, believe me. No doubt about it, I'm definitely different. And I'm gonna make it my mission to share the wealth. Gonna go out into the world and teach every lesson I've learned. And believe me, believe me, in twenty-two years, you sure learn a lot.

HAROLD
any age
Dramatic

Harold recalls an early childhood memory.

(A gentle memory.) Moonlight, shadows on the ceiling. Almost asleep. Then it would start, as usual, every Friday night. Just as I was dozing, the davening would begin, from the synagogue across the street. The men, together, praying. Then the cantor would start singing; his deep, glorious voice filled my room with warm, comforting tones. Then soon the rest of the congregation would gently join in; like good-night lullabies. Their warm cries, tender voices, flooded my room. Their shadows surrounded me, circling me in my bed. I was a kid, awake but asleep. They'd come to protect, shield me. And now nothing, no one, could get in. My room was sealed. And soon the ceiling would disappear, and the walls would fall away. Dark, night, but I wasn't afraid, not anymore. Safe . . . finally . . . Friday. It was dark and night time was here. And I was in bed, almost, almost asleep. It was Friday, another Friday night — and the rabbis were here.

MEMPHIS
adult
Dramatic

Memphis, a homeless man, tells a man about a murder he's just seen.

I know, realize I'm not makin' much sense here. But it's true, it is, I swear. She was just a kid, and he killed her. This man, he murdered that little girl. And her mother didn't do nothin', just sat there. Just sat there by the train tracks, DIDN'T MOVE, DIDN'T HELP, NOTHIN'!

At first I thought maybe I'm sleepin', maybe it's a dream. Or maybe I'm still drunk; s'just the booze. So I kept rollin' my head around like this, slappin' my face hard as I could, sayin', "Wake up, Memphis, you dreamin' man, this here's a nightmare!" But that man, he kept hittin' her, that little black girl, and she kept screamin', and I knew it was no fuckin' dream, no. Could feel it, felt every slap, every punch, every kick. Was like that man, he was hittin' me. Was like he was beatin' me up. And shit, I been beat before, so I know how it feels. Been beat up plenty, so I know how it hurts. But he wasn't hittin' me, no, was hittin' her. So tiny, so small. And him so big. Unfair, unfair! And I couldn't move, was like paralyzed. My legs wouldn't work. Couldn't scream neither, no. Couldn't yell, call a cop. Couldn't make a sound, nothin'! Just air comin' out of my mouth. Just air, I swear! And her mother sat there like she didn't hear her daughter cryin'; like she didn't know or see! Like she was blind and deaf! Then suddenly it got quiet, real quiet. That little girl stopped cryin', didn't move no more. Then her mother got up, went over, looked down at her daughter, started to cry. Cried so loud that lady. Was like she'd been savin' up that cry for her whole life. Then the man, he left; walked away. Went down the train tracks. Then the girl's mother left, ran after him. And she caught up, and soon the two of them just sort of — disappeared. And then I could move again, went to where that little girl was, looked down, saw what he done.

(A beat.) Come with me, mister. Come and I'll show you where she is, what he did. Come with me to the railroad tracks, and I'll show you what happened. This was no dream, no. You come, you come, you'll see.

STAN

adult
Serio-comedic

Stan, a man who was at one time going to be a preacher, lectures to his students about his loss of faith.

Such a delicate thing, faith. It can dissolve, disappear, in an instant. Needs nurturing, hope, to survive. I don't know how many of you know this, but I was going to be a preacher once. *(Smiling.)* Me, imagine, a preacher. Was all I thought about, my biggest dream. But then I woke up one morning and found I'd lost my faith. It was gone, disappeared, wasn't there. Gone, like Peter Pan's shadow. I— became frantic, started searching everywhere; under the bed, in my closet, under my pillow! My faith had fled and I felt — hollow. Well, who'd hire a preacher without faith? "Life's what happens while you're making other plans." That was a long time ago. I've been searching ever since. I teach, I lecture, I learn.

The thing that still connects me to God is my anger, my anger, yeah. See, what I see all around me enrages me. The world . . . well, just pick and choose, it's not a pretty picture. And odd as it might seem, I'm angry at God for all those things that make me angry. See, to me, faith means *challenging* God. I can't be angry at something that doesn't exist, right? So what I'm saying here, what I'm trying to say, is my *rage* fortifies my faith! I mean if there's no God, then what the hell have I got to be angry about, right?! Mean I could just lie down, play dead, and wait for it all. . . . But I'm a FIGHTER, and I prefer. . . . So on any given day, I'll stand there, angry as hell, fist to sky, screaming, yelling! And while ranting, RAVING, like a god-damned lunatic, I often discover, almost by accident . . . !

(*Softer.*) That despite my loss of faith, I'm still, still — a very — religious — man.

MICKEY
fifty and older
Dramatic

Mickey, a middle-aged drag queen tenderly reflects while standing on a empty night-club stage.

(Softly.) Standing out here like this, in the quiet, in the dark, it's my favorite time. Gives me solace, gets me centered. Memories, old times. I like to come out here on the stage every night before all the craziness begins. Just sit, look out, and listen — to nothing. So soothing, so serene. So . . . temporary. I know once I go back in there, this calm will be shattered; showtime. And my little divas-in-waiting will give me their biggest smiles, most playful curtsies. Respect, reverence, "Mama Rose" has entered. And I'll give my regal wave, smile demurely, sit at my table, begin my toilette; while listening to their endless sorority girl chatter. To their camping, dishing, sordid stories of who's hot and who's not — and oh God, do I remember? Same song, different verse. Then we'll get into our dresses, check out our makeup, throw on our heels. And old Harry'll call "Five minutes! Last looks, girls." And my heart'll start pounding like it's the first time. My mouth will get dry, and I'll worry, do I know my words? Then wonder, where are we tonight, Provincetown, Key West? But then I'll relax as I realize it really doesn't matter. Same songs, different club, same steps. And the boys will always be boys, and the show never changes. And there's still some fizz left in the old champagne.

(A beat, taking it all in.) Standing out here, alone in the quiet, in the dark, it's my favorite time.

TIMOTHY

any age
Comedic

Timothy works for a very prestigious company. But here he admits to a major indiscretion that may affect his future.

(*Sincerely apologetic.*) I admit it, I did it, I'm sorry. She promised to be discreet, sir. She promised, she swore, I believed her. I'm so, so sorry, sir.

I met her at a party at my friend Paul's. We had a few drinks, started to talk. And I couldn't help but notice she was quite an eyeful. And it was obvious she was interested. Well the talk soon turned to sex, the conversation became arousing. And well, I'm a man, I admit it, my mind was floating in the gutter. She asked if I wanted to leave; felt like I'd won the lottery. We flew back to her place, had a few, well, several more drinks. And that's when my judgment, I guess, got cloudy. She was very, very seductive, sir. Told me to get undressed, which I did, immediately. There was some erotic music, a few more drinks, a little dance, dim lighting, some hot wax, a naked kiss, and then . . . out came the camera. Funny, I don't remember there being a flash. Barely remember rolling around on the rug like that; didn't realize I was so limber. Just remember her looking down, taking pictures, me getting all giggly, and her yelling orders. I really don't remember signing that release, but that is my signature, sir. Proof's in the pudding, the pictures are on the page.

Sir, I realize this doesn't reflect well on me or the company. Especially in "that" kind of magazine. I mean that kind of magazine certainly doesn't reflect my sexual preference. What concerns me now is what happens next. This company means a great deal to me, sir. I hope to have a future here. And those pictures, well, I hope you won't hold them against me. I mean I hope I won't be too severely — penalized.

JOHN
any age
Dramatic

John gratefully talks to his rescuer.

Safe, safer, thank you. I feel safe here with you. It's been, well you know, a nightmare. Thank you for rescuing me. That hallway was so goddamned dark. I was lost, wandering like some Moses in a dark desert: debris everywhere. Couldn't find a staircase, nothing. Smoke, dark, dirt. So there I was walking, well, crawling on the floor, wondering if I'd ever . . . ? Then I just stood up, yeah. Covered my ears, stomped my feet, yelled, "Do not cry. Do not cry!" Hit my fists against some wall or . . . "Should be ashamed!," that's what my grandma used to say, "Should be ashamed of yourself for being such a baby!" Grandma was a tower of strength. Then out of nowhere, a hand, a voice, a word. Well actually two, you said, "You okay?" Help had arrived, the cavalry had come! *(Smiling.)* Thank you, thank you for rescuing me *(Looking around.)* And now, here I am. *(A big smile.)* HERE I ARE! Safe; out of harm's way. And it's *not* the end of the goddamned world. I have survived. I am safe, right? Right, mister?

(He suddenly stops. Realizing.) Mister?

(Becoming frightened, looking around, calling.) Hello?! HELLO?!

(Louder.) Anyone here? Anyone here?!

HENRY

any age
Serio-comedic

Here Henry, an "artist" talks pointedly to a fellow artist.

(With an edge.)
    I see you.
    I know you.
    I know you're there.
    I don't have to look,
    no, it's not necessary.
    I know you're there, that's all.
        People like you always are.
        Sitting, waiting, anticipating. Hoping,
no praying — for my failure.
We put our work up here.
                Tell what we have to tell.
                Say what we have to say.
We show and tell our wares.
                It's what we do, yes.
                And
                you . . .
        secretly hide out there.
        Feign friendship,
        put on a smile,
        pretend we're good pals,
        just one of the gals.
    You silently hide in the dark,
                run to your God,
                pray for the failure
                of me and my "art."

(A whisper.)
    "Cassius," lean, hungry Cassius can you hear me?

    We all attempt,
            try to tell our truth.
    We want,
            no need,
                someone to say,
        "You're talented,
            I believe in you!"
(A whisper.)
    We need that, "Monsieur Salierri,"
                yes, we do.
                        Me,
                    as well as you.
We're both victims of that same nasty need.
                So — sit there in the dark.
                Put me down,
                hate me, hate my art.
                Wish me the worst if you will.
        Perhaps you even hope me terminally ill.
        But you're wasting your time,
                    you are.
            Don't you know?
            Can't you tell?
                    I can see in the dark.
                    Can't you can see it in my
                    eyes?
            Stop pretending.
            I'm bathing in your despise.
            Haven't you guessed yet?
            It's obvious.
            And obvious is true.

I've sat there,
judging,
just like you.

Resenting;
sitting in the same seat,
the same dark,
hating you,
belittling
your art.

So hey-hey,
what they hell,
let's lift a glass,
have a toast to hate!
Savor it!
Hope it spurs us on to better things.
Kinder thoughts,
more moral themes.
We're both two sides of the same coin.
It's obvious;
and obvious is true.
I've sat there.
I know you.
And now,
hey-hey,
now you
know me too.

MURRAY
adult
Serio-comedic

Murray, a teacher, lectures to his students about the commandment, "Honor thy parents."

(With a building fervor.) Middle of the desert! Moses, top of Mount Sinai, a hot day; things are happening. *(A little joke.)* The Ten Commandments, the original, not the movie. And God has just uttered number five of the top-fab-ten, "Honor thy parents." Well according to the scriptures, God created this commandment because our parents gave us the glorious gift of life. The thirteenth-century "Book of Mitzvah Education" explains that by honoring one's parents, a person will recognize the goodness of God. Parents, God, goodness. In Kiddushin 31a of the Talmud, there's a story of a mother spitting in her son's face, and the son nonetheless continues to accord her honor. And even though she had insulted him, he continued to love and revere her.

(A momentum starting.) So if a parent neglected you, should you still honor them? Well according . . . The Ten Commandments say very clearly, "Honor thy parents"! Mr. Webster defines "honor" as " a person of superior standing. One whose worth brings respect. Homage, reverence, love."

(Continuing, getting worked up.) BUT if they abused you, neglected you, didn't give you the love you needed, secretly craved, HOW can you honor, love them now? What I'm saying . . .

(Continuing, louder.) What I'm trying to say . . . !

There's a deficit! A deficit exists, inside; and everything you . . . Everyone you'll ever meet . . . ! A deficit . . . a deficit exists! And so . . . so forgiving, forgetting . . . ? I mean just let it go, right? Was a long time ago. They did the best they could, right? Right! Your parents tried, they tried, so turn the other cheek! And honor? Create it any way you can! Out of clay if you have to! Out of . . .

(Getting frustrated, searching.) I'm going somewhere with all this, just stay with me. —Honor! Parents! God! But at the end of the day . . . What you'll discover . . . What I've . . . !

(Frustrated, to himself.) Shit.

(Continuing.) You always go home. You look, will always be looking . . . ! Will always . . . !

(He stops. Then, looking out at his students. Almost a plea.)

Where do you go to fill the hollow, the deficit? Where do you go to find the missing love?

(Pulling himself together.) According . . . The Ten Commandments . . . Ten Commandments say very clearly, Honor . . . thy . . . parents!

NEIL
forty and older
serio-comedic

Here Neil recalls a traumatic night he spent with his best friends years earlier.

Remember? I was a fuckin' mess. Called you, and you said come on up. Ran here to Boston, met you at the airport. The look in your eyes that night, I'll never forget. We caught a cab, went to that dive downtown, got drunk, remember? Tequilas, Cuervo, salt on the rim. And you sat there, listened, as I emptied her out of me. "How could she fuckin' walk out on me?! That bitch, who the hell does she . . . ?!" And you sat there, just sat there, let me talk. Then you talked, well tried to talk, I was too drunk, wouldn't let ya. Then we both started talkin' at the same time, remember? Yellin', screamin, shit, we were drunk! Then they threw us out, remember? A big scene, something about a salt shaker or something, I forgot. Then dinner at Dubrows, dessert first, remember? We thought that was hysterical, dessert first. Laughed, yeah laughed. Then it came, the tears. Cryin' her the hell out of me; and you sat there, listened, just listened. Just like always. Listening, letting me talk.

(A beat.) Well, shit, water under the bridge You know she's been married twice now, you know that? Kids are both graduating college this year. Time. Yeah. Sure flies. . . . I just . . . You saved my life that night, you know that? Don't know what I woulda done. Was nowhere left. I called and you said, "Come on up. Come on up, just like always. And I always meant to . . . It all boils down to . . .

"Thank you. Thank you for being my friend. For always being there." Means more than you can imagine.

(An awkward beat.) Okay, so . . . what you gonna have? Hear the halibut's good here. S'fresh, comes in from Gloucester. Order whatever you like. Tonight . . . this one's on me.

DON

any age
Dramatic

Here Don recalls the day his father left and the impact it had on his life.

(A somber memory.) Doors and windows. Leaving and looking out. Windows, walls, and doors. Our family had broken up, my father had left. Every family's got its freak shows, its runaways. Someone leaving, someone looking out, someone left behind. Something better, somewhere else. He just left, no good-byes, nothing. He left our home, windows, walls, and doors.

I didn't see him for almost twenty years; his hospital room, the day he died. Oh I'd call, sure, the good son, the occasional long distance, "How you doing, Dad?" Short conversations about nothing. Then I'd hang up, forget him for a while, erase, for long stretches. But then a scene in a movie would remind me. Or a song on the radio. Or a thought while driving to some bar late at night. A nagging memory . . . of something that never was.

So then you enter the bar, look around, lose yourself in all the unfamiliar faces. A smile, a nod, a drink. Stares, looks. You listen to the music, sip on your drink, wait; hope, think. Then maybe a few more drinks, just to loosen up. But sooner or later, you still find yourself, even after all these years, wondering, what if? Remembering, thinking about what might have been.

HAMILTON
Any age
Serio-comedic

Hamilton talks about the excitement of stealing from his mother.

I could cough right on cue. *(He coughs.)* At just the right time, just the right moment. See I knew if I timed it just right, the cough could cover the sound of the click. But after the cough and click I was in; her pocketbook was opened. And there was her change purse staring straight up at me. Then another cough *(He coughs again.)*, another click, and the change purse was opened! And inside, inside, were all her coins and bills. How much could I take without her missing any? How much could I get away with? I quickly grabbed a handful, put 'em in my pocket. Then grabbed another. Then coughed *(He does.)*, closed her change purse. Then coughed *(He does.)*, closed her pocketbook. Then tiptoed out of her room as quietly as I could. Walked by the kitchen, saw her cooking, said "How much longer till supper, Ma?" And she'd say "A few minutes more, go get washed." And I'd run to my room, hide the cash. And all through dinner I'd sit there, smile, and eat. I'd finish everything off my plate, everything! Then I'd run down to the candy store, fast as I could, and buy lots and lots of candy! Good and plenty, M & M's, Milky Ways. All kinds, every flavor! Then I sat on the curb on the corner and ate it all. Savor *every single piece!* Till finally, finally I was filled. I mean really filled; I mean stuffed to the gills! . . . And then I'd get up, go back home, go to my room, to the bathroom, to the toilet, get down on my knees, and throw it all up; empty out, all of it. Till finally I was no longer filled. Till finally I was no longer — stuffed to the gills.

JAY

adult

Serio-comedic

Jay, a bartender, talks about his infidelity.

I was working here round the clock, busting my chops, try-ing to provide, be a good husband. Got her a new fur coat, nice car, you name it. But finally, frustrated, I thought, "Fuck this, I got needs, y'know?" And my wife's not ful-filling them. I mean how much can you put up with, right?! So innocently, and I mean that, in all honesty, *inno-cently,* I discovered, almost by accident, that this bar can be an oasis, a kind of candy store. I mean, they come in here all day, all the little lovelies. A little lonely, order a drink, want someone to talk to. And me, hey, I'm a walk-ing confessional booth. So I serve 'em, listen, let 'em talk, let 'em know I care. Let 'em know "I'm here for you," talk to me, Daddy. Come sit on my knee. Then pretty soon, dosey-doe, one thing leads *(Smiling.),* well, y'know. Then off we go, magic carpet rides, visits to the Milky Way. Then after, a wink good-bye, pat on the butt, quick kiss, and everyone's happy, everyone's — satisfied. Home is where the heart is. Yeah. Home is . . . *(Smiling.)* Anyplace I hang my hat — is home.

JACK
adult
Dramatic

Here Jack tenderly remembers his best friend.

Minute I met him I knew. Wasn't hard to tell; I mean his eyes were going in two different directions, his speech was slurred, he wobbled a bit and asked me if I was Jesus. Figured either he was stoned or psychotic. At first I was a little, y'know, "This guy could be dangerous." But as we talked, I realized he was just tripping. I mean it was the seventies, shit, everybody was tripping back then on something. And I liked him, I did. Took a chance, figure'd it'd be fine. Took him out to Fire Island with me. And we sat on the beach that night and just talked, talked, talked. He told me about his life, I told him about mine. Discovered we had a lot in common; him the lapsed Catholic, me the fallen Jew. We became fast friends, best friends — never lovers. Always made each other laugh. Good times; talk, talk, talk. Traveled together, shared secrets, talked trash, last night's tricks, long phone calls, holidays, double dates, dreams, dramas, best friends: friendship! Years past, memories, moments you never forget.

Then came the eighties, remember the eighties? Wow, an explosion! Drugs, sex — and well, along with a lot of others — I got AIDS. *(Building in intensity.)* Then we really talked, talked, talked. When I got sicker, he went to the doctors with me, and we'd talk, talk, talk. And I got sicker, so he took care of me; talk, talk, talk! Pick a subject, A to Z, talk, talk, talk! I got sicker, he moved in, TALK, TALK, TALK! Tell me a joke, make me laugh — TALK,

TALK, TALK! And I got sicker — we TALKED! And sicker — we TALKED! AND SICKER — WE TALKED! AND SICKER — TALKED, TALKED, TALKED!!

(A beat, softer.) One Sunday morning, while he was still asleep in a chair by my bed, I left the room, I died. Friends, best friends. Nothing left to say . . . everything was said.

BART

any age
Comedic

While standing in a crowded subway, Bart encounters a beautiful young girl.

She was standing next to me, right next to me there in the subway. It was crowded, rush hour, and the air conditioning was on the fritz. So it was hot, sweaty. And she's standing close, I mean CLOSE, almost on top of me. Then she turned, looked at me, sort of smiled. And she's beautiful this girl, young, maybe twenty, twenty two, tops. Maybe Mexican, middle Eastern, something like that. And there was this look in her eyes; no doubt about it, *(Smiling.)* SHIT YEAH, I KNEW! The subway stops start flying by, and I'm trying to figure out what should I say? What should I do?! As she's pressing tightly up against me. I mean I can smell her perfume, feel her fingers. Finally I figure why bother with words? It's obvious what she wants, take it for what it's worth. I couldn't believe that this was happening, right there in the subway! *(Smiling.)* So I closed my eyes, let her have "her way" with me. I'm her boy-toy right there in the subway. The stops are flying by, and I'm totally enjoying the ride; amazed that no one else in the car even knew. All those poor bastards, sweating, suffering, while I'm off on some tropical island, being pampered, touched, stroked. Finally, we get to Forty-second Street. The crowd starts emptying out; there's a shift, a shove, and she disappears. I quickly look through the window, see her. She sort of smiles, I smile back, . . . and then she's gone.

Gone . . . with my wallet and my watch. Didn't take long to figure out. After adjusting my suit, I felt in my pocket, then looked down at my wrist. Oh no. Shit, yeah . . . I knew.

JOSH
adult
Dramatic

Josh recalls the deep religious feelings he had when he was a child.

Saturdays, Shabbos, in shul. Faded white tallit and dark black yamulkas. I was just a fat little kid among the men. An almost member of the congregation. Each of us alone, but all of us together; Jews, davening. Constant movement, bending and swaying. Looking towards the Torah, praying from our hearts. It was the orthodox synagogue, a few blocks from my house. I'd go there every Saturday morning. The old rabbi would always smile at me, a wink, a nod, approval. Good boy, good Jew. It was there, in shul that I knew. Seemed like it was the only place that I was ever certain about anything. Maybe I didn't have the right words or proof; just faith, my feelings.

(Continuing, building in joyful intensity.) I knew He was here. I could feel it! He was in the bright candle light, in the stained glass windows; in every wooden pew, in the dark cries of the canter on the high holy holidays. I could feel it, I could! He was in the old siddur books, in the opening of the Torah, the sound of our voices, the look in our eyes; the dedication, devotion! I could feel it, I was sure! I was certain!

(A beat, softer.) And then when the service was over, I'd say my good-byes, go home, go to my room, sit on my bed, look out the window, imagine what my life would be like when I became a rabbi, a rebbe, me. Black hat, black

coat, long beard, glasses. Respected, honored, loved. The wise old rabbi, with his own congregation.

But then, I'd hear them, my mother and father in the other room, yelling, cursing, "You son of a bitch!" this, "You bastard!" that. Fights, battles, arguments. I'd cover my ears, close my eyes; until finally their voices disappeared. And I'd lie back in bed, look out my window, and wonder where was God — now?

RICHARD

adult

Dramatic

Richard, a gay man, recalls a night of sex he had when he was younger.

My mind was wandering. Gone, other worlds, places you only dream of. So there I was that night, making love to this boy on the beach, and suddenly my mind went flying, became unfocused. Heard him calling me, this boy, from miles below. "Hey you up there, what's happenin'? Knock three times if you're still alive." A laugh, some giggles in the dark. But I was lost somewhere in the jet stream, imagining a whole different scenario between us. You see, I assumed, believed, that this boy . . . That we were both on the same track, "romance automatic"; me above, him below. I believed back then that you could never think too loud, or talk too soft when you were in love. That there'd be, was allowed to be, a loving silence, a quiet something you shared with someone in the dark. Words . . . words unnecessary. I heard them talk about it in movies, sing about it in love songs. And so what I thought was happening, what I was imagining . . . But no, I was just drunk. Or stoned on pot or on pills. And so was he if memory serves. So no, we weren't . . . No, not love, not even — close. It was just sex. Good old-fashioned, beach-blanket bingo, hot times, summer in the city, sex! Two kids, cold, late night, stoned, wind in our hair, sand in every pore, Mamas and Papas playing on his transistor radio, surf's up, Brighton Beach, down and dirty, under the boardwalk, Brooklyn-style sex! Sex, and it was good! Sex, and it was great!! Sex, and it was safe!! . . . But that was then, and this is now. And now that boy he's barely even a memory. I have no idea who he was or where . . . . Or even . . . And the oceans are polluted today. And the sands on the beaches of Brooklyn are now filled with debris, tin cans, and used colored condoms. I'm only telling you all this because . . . I don't know, because my mind just momentarily fell back into focus. A snapshot, a memory, a pornographic picture from the past fell into my lap. And just like that memory, this moment too shall evaporate, eventually.

MIKE
adult
Comedic

Mike, an abusive husband, yells at his wife, who is threatening to leave him.

What, what'd you just say? What I thought, what I thought you said, tell me if I'm wrong, was that you're *leaving?!* No, I don't think so. That's not gonna happen; not here, not now, not ever! Door swings one way, bitch, and that's *in.* Now put that suitcase back and bring me a beer. D'cha hear me?! A beer! Then I'll tell you about the day I had, shit I had to put up with. Then you can do your boo-hoo about vacuum cleaning and how hard it is doin' dishes. You live a charmed life, bitch, believe me, while I'm out there bustin' my balls, trying to pay the bills! Now go get me a Bud! . . . Why you still standing there? You deaf? No one's leavin' here, ya hear? Not tonight, not tomorrow, not ever! I am the husband, this is my home, those are my orders! Now put-the-god-damned-bags-back-in-the-bedroom, bitch, and bring me a beer! . . . DID YOU HEAR ME! *(She doesn't do it.)* Hey, hey, what I gotta do, beg? Put 'em back. *(She doesn't.)* Put 'em back! *(Stamping his foot.)* PUT-THEM-BACK! *(She dosen't, a beat, softer.)* Okay, all right, put 'em back — please. *(Softening.)* Please, c'mon; I said please. Please put 'em back. *(She doesn't, gentler.)* . . . All right, look, I'm sorry. I'm sorry, okay? Sorry I called you a bitch; wasn't nice. And we can just forget about the beer, I'm not thirsty anymore. Now why don't you come over here, sit down, and we'll order out Chinese? *(She doesn't.)* C'mon, c'mon, you love Chinese; we'll order spare ribs, sweet and sour pork. *(Sweeter.)* . . . Honey, what's wrong? What? Tell me, I'm all ears. C'mon, I wanna know; really, really. *(Opening his arms to her, lovingly.)* . . . C'mon, c'mon, baby, come to Daddy, tell me. Please. . . . Pleeeease!

MICHAEL
any age
Dramatic

Michael tells his brother about the moment he became aware that he had AIDS.

I kept hoping, y'know? Kept . . . But I knew, I just . . . I was losing weight, tired all the time. Mom kept saying, "Mickey, you're getting so thin. What's wrong?" Telling her it's just stress, don't worry, Ma. Telling myself it's this or that. Anything, any excuse, one after another. But then I ran out of reasons; there were no excuses left. So finally I went to the doctor.

Then last night, sitting there in the waiting room — forever. Making all kinds of deals with myself. Promises, y'know. If only . . . anything . . . I'll be good. But when he came in, was walking towards me, the look in his eyes, Barry. I'll never forget. The game was over. The doctor didn't have to say a thing — I knew.

JEREMY

any age
Dramatic

Jeremy tucks his young son into bed and says good night.

(Tenderly.)
Well son,
      that's it,
            that's all he had to say;
                end of story.
Time for sleep.
The fire's out,
      The thunder stopped,
            the lion sleeps tonight.
Now go to sleep, boy.
      Go ahead.
And dream wonderful dreams.
            And don't be afraid of the dark.
            There's nothing to be afraid of anymore;
            no.
'Cause when you wake up,
      I promise,
            it'll be light;
               a sunshiny day.
One-brand-new-day-coming-up for my boy!
      And maybe Mommy will be back, maybe.
And we'll all go to the zoo
      like we use to.
And play together, and have lots and lots of fun.

Together,
        just like we use to;
maybe.
Maybe,
        tomorrow
                we'll see.

Now close your eyes, boy,
        go to sleep,
                and dream some wonderful dreams.
I'll just turn off the light here.
Shhhh, shhh, sleep.
(A beat, he looks at his son, softly.)
Daddy loves you.
        Yes he does.
Daddy loves you,
        yes.

MURRAY

Adult
Serio-comedic

Murray, a college professor of Jewish studies, lectures to his new students about God.

God. Three letters, one word. In Hebrew, Adonai, El Shaddai, or Elohim. What? Why do some of you look so surprised? C'mon, c'mon, you knew this one was coming. This is it, the lecture about God. We've got to talk about him. He's what this course is all about. Think about it, just think about it; when all else fails, when your plane hits turbulence, when someone holds a gun to your head — "God, help me"! When you're lonely, need someone to lean on, when your life's flying out of control! For whatever reason, even if you don't think you believe, you go to God.

The purpose of this course, which I've been teaching since last millennium, is NOT to come to any conclusions. Here we begin the never-ending process of not ever finding out. I only ask you all to commit, come to class. Then any questions you have, ask. Answers not guaranteed. As you can tell, I have a tendency to talk a lot, sorry, bear with me. *(A smile.)* I'm taking this course too, I'm still trying to pass. What I hope is that by the end of the term, each one of you will walk away with some "excellent questions." So be smart, not lazy and listen. Every once in a while I may just say something . . . Look, this isn't a required course, so I assume you're all here because you want to be. Well, one bit of advice. If you really want to find out, learn something, you've got to be willing to toss a few rocks aside, burrow a bit.

Okay, that's it. . . . Today we'll talk about the Talmud, the collected book of Jewish knowledge. But first up, as previously mentioned, the main man, man in charge — God.

Got any questions yet? . . . Good. 'Cause I know I've got plenty.

SEYMOUR
middle aged and older
Dramatic

Seymour's wife has recently died. He tenderly remembers their love.

At first it was just tongue, tease, loving looks, and red, red lipstick. Man, I was biting at the bit on a daily basis. We'd just started dating, but soon we fell in love; then the war came. I was drafted. Sad good-byes, lots of tears, long-lasting kisses. We wrote letters, lots and lots of love letters. Her letters kept me going over there. She was all I'd think about. Then the day I got back, I'll never forget, way she looked, standing there in front of her stoop; flowered dress, barrette in her hair; her wave, her smile. We ran, kissed, held each other. Was like a scene from a movie. Was right then and there I knew, she was the one. Soon we got married, big wedding, everyone, everyone from the avenue was there. You shoulda seen. Plans, hopes, dreams. We had our honeymoon in Miami, was magical. Long walks on the beach, kisses in the moonlight, holding hands. She said she wanted a few kids, I said, "Sure, fine." Plans, hopes, dreams. Said she wanted to live out at Brighton Beach. I said "Honey, anywhere, long as it's with you." See I'd never loved anyone like that. Never felt those kind of feelings; never. Never before, never since. She was . . . my everything! Plans . . . hopes . . . dreams.

BRIAN

any age
Comedic

Brian, a gay man, recalls some of the trials and tribulations of childbirth.

We'd wanted a child for so long. So finally one night I told him, "Yeah, sure, let's do it!" And all I can say is I knew. Knew it that night. We were making love, the moon was full. It was warm, John was gentle. And after, I remember looking up at old Mr. Moon, winking, then falling asleep, knowing, I knew.

When the doctor gave us the good news, that I was, you know, with child, I jumped into Johnny's arms. We both ran out of the office, giving all the hopefuls in the waiting room a big thumbs up. We were going to have a baby, boy oh boy!

Those first few months, well, all I can say is me and Mr. Toilet Bowl became very good friends. Of course there was my vanity. Had my *physique* to consider, didn't want to blow up like a balloon. I continued going to the gym, working out. Every once in a while, one of the guys would mention my new "beer gut." I'd just smile, say "Yeah, gotta watch them brewskies!"

Sometimes at night, while we'd be watching TV, Johnny would ask if he could listen to the baby. I'd let him put his ear to my belly. He'd start yelling, "He's kicking!" I'd smile, but always thought it was just gas.

Pretty soon I was showing, it was apparent. Anyone who looked, saw, knew. People in crowds on the street would separate for me when I'd come by. Old men on buses gave me their seats. Handicapped people limped out of my way. I'd smile, a gracious, natal thank you. I discovered that the world is much kinder to those with child.

As my due date approached, John and I would practice our hospital exit routine every day. It was during one of those practice runs that something terrible happened. John, well, he never saw that car coming. All I remember is the look on his face as he flew up into the air; higher and higher! Oh, no! Higher and higher! I screamed, as John finally came down with a crash. We rushed him to the hospital. Was touch and go for days, but they said he was going to make it.

That last stretch of my pregnancy was filled with lots of lonely nights. John was still in the hospital. Was just me all alone, staring up at old Mr. Moon. But the neighbors, my friends, and some family helped out. When the day came, everything went perfectly. But the very best part was in the delivery room. I was in labor, contractions, was terrible. When from nowhere, they wheeled my Johnny in. He was in a cast up to his neck, tubes coming in and out of him, and his mouth was wired shut so he couldn't talk. But with every ounce of strength he gave me a big thumbs up! Thumbs up to you too, Johnny.

(Smiling, proudly.)

Well, our baby boy was born a few hours later; eight pounds, three ounces. And like everyone says when they see him, John Junior, our little boy, has got his fathers' face.

NED

adult
Dramatic

Ned tells his memory about his mother to a psychiatrist.

The bathroom door was slightly opened. I could see in, saw them, but they didn't see me. Some steam from a hot tub was drifting out, like a mysterious cloud. She was standing in the light in front of the mirror, in her white bra and panties, putting on her makeup. The way the light lit her, my mother looked . . . magical, like a movie star. My father was standing right behind her, close, touching, his hand over her shoulder, gently caressing her breast in her clean white bra. He was sweating, she was not. The look in his eyes . . . I was young, but I understood. She continued putting on her makeup. It seemed . . . was almost like he wasn't there, like he didn't even exist. He kissed the back of her shoulder, her neck, the side of her face. Suddenly she stopped putting on her makeup. Was like she'd just realized that he was even in the room. She was annoyed; a cold glaze; an angry look. She pushed his hand away. He quickly put it back on her breast, started kissing her again, rubbing up against her. She slapped his hand hard, very hard! I felt, could feel that slap. He glared at her in the mirror. She stared back. The two of them stood there, frozen, looking straight ahead. I was young, but I understood. He cursed at her, then left. I ran to my room. I heard the bathroom door slam, got into my bed, under the covers. Then the front door slammed; he was gone. It was quiet again, just the sound of the ocean outside, the waves. And I stayed hidden in my warm blanket hideaway till finally I fell asleep. And I dreamt, doctor, about my mother, in the bathroom, in her clean white bra and panties. And she looked beautiful, so beautiful, just like a movie star. And she was admiring herself in the mirror, putting on her makeup. But in my dream, in my dream, I was there too, standing right behind her; close, touching, just the two of us looking straight ahead into the steam-filled mirror. And we were both smiling, both very happy. And then, in my dream, the bathroom door slowly closed.

GARY

any age
Dramatic

Shortly after his wife died, a mysterious stranger moved into his home. Here Gary recalls his relationship with the stranger. This monologue is a meditation on grief.

(A painful memory.) He moved in shortly after she died. Perhaps not right away, but soon. We never spoke, had nothing to say. He went his way, I went mine. Days, weeks, maybe months. We kept our distance, never saw each other. He'd stay in his room, I remained in mine. The house was quiet during that time, very quiet. It was usually dark, perhaps a light lit late at night, I don't quite remember. I do remember people coming by, but I can't recall anything they said. They'd come, they'd visit, then go. Sometimes late at night, while I was trying to sleep, I heard him crying. I thought I did, but I'm not sure. I'd just lie there, listen, till finally I'd fall asleep. Perhaps I should I have comforted him, but I couldn't. I'd lie there, hear him, see her, remember. Days, weeks, maybe months.

Then one night I heard three knocks on my wall. I thought I was just imagining it. But then I heard three more knocks. I immediately went to his room, knocked on his door, entered, asked him if he was all right. It was dark in there, very, very dark. It was the the darkest room I'd ever been in. He was sitting alone on his bed. I sat next to him. Neither of us said a word. Silent echoes. And then — I started to talk. I began telling him all about her. About the wonderful times we had shared. About our love, our wonderful life together. And he listened and would occasionally smile. And I smiled, for the first time in a long time. And I talked and talked all through the night. I clutched his hand tightly. I wanted, needed to be certain that he'd never forget, never, for the rest of his life. The room filled with a soft haze.

When the sun came up the next morning, I was sitting there, my hands clasped, alone. Of course. Of course I was. All along, all alone. I opened the blinds, looked out. The alarm clock rang, the sun was shining. It was the beginning of a new day.

SAM

adult
Comedic

Sam joyfully recalls the day his son was born.

(Joyfully.)
We were waiting in the waiting room, Sadie and me. Had been there for hours, driving each other nuts. Finally, the nurse comes out, big smile, calls me over, and says, "You his father?"
"His? Father?! YES!!"
"Healthy baby boy!," she says, "Healthy baby boy."

It's a boy, BOOM, it's a boy!
"I've got a son," I say to Sadie. "I got a son!"

Sadie and me hug and kiss.
"Mazel tov, mazel tov!"

The nurse brings him out.
And let me tell ya,
let me tell you, the first
time you see your son,
NOTHIN' matches that!
A miracle!

(Joyfully.)
This fat, little, butterball.
Little fingers, little toes.
Ya get emotional!
Sadie starts to cry, nurse starts to laugh.

"S'my son!," I say to Sadie. "S'my son!
"S'my grandson," she boasts, "My grandson!"
I'm handing out cigars, pissin' in my pants.
Sadie starts to laugh, I start to cry.

Mazel tov! Mazel tov!
Little fingers, little hands.
You feel so . . . ! You feel . . . !
(Softly, smiling.)
What a god-damned day that was . . .
what a goddamned day!

MARK
adult
Comedic

Mark has become obsessed with a strange woman he met at a club downtown.

It's crazy. I know, I know it sounds crazy. But I'll prove it, you'll see! Don't look at me like that, PLEASE, I'm not nuts! . . . Her name's Mary, Mary, and I met her at a club downtown, a few weeks ago. Was a rainy night, I was lonely, she was standing by the bar. And all I can say was that from the minute our eyes made contact, I was SMIT-TEN! She walked over, said hello. We danced, hardly say-ing a word; just deep, dark stares. Then we went back to my place, made love, and it was like NOTHING I'd ever experienced! It was like dreaming, surreal; touching, tast-ing, biting. Then a deep, dark sleep. When I awoke, Mary was gone. Left me a note asking me to meet her at the club that night. I felt totally drained all day, but all I could think about was Mary. Then that night, minute I met her, the same magic! And again we went back to my place, and it was even BETTER than the night before! More brutal, devouring, more delicious! I've seen her every night since. And every morning, doctor, I'm more drained. She's . . . she's very dangerous, doctor. I'm afraid. When I look in the mirror in the morning, they're there; the little mementos of Mary. *(He rolls down his shirt collar.)* Here, see, see them? These little holes on my neck? I know what they are. I know what she is. I know what she's doing to me. But I was lonely, and now, now I'm not. *(Undoing the collar even more.)* Here, look, look, doctor, you tell me. Go ahead, tell me if you think I'm crazy — or just crazy in love.

Smith and Kraus
SPECIAL INTEREST MONOLOGUES

2 Minutes and Under: Character Monologues for Actors By Glenn Alterman

100 True Soliloquies for Men Ed. by Jennie Wyckoff

100 True Soliloquies for Women Ed. by Jennie Wyckoff

The Great Monologues from the EST Marathon Ed. by Kristin Graham

The Great Monologues from the Humana Festival Ed. by Kristin Graham

The Great Monologues from the Mark Taper Forum Ed. by Kristin Graham

The Great Monologues from the Women's Project Ed. by Kristin Graham

Ice Babies in Oz: Character Monologues For Actors By L.E. McCullough

Monologues from Contemporary Literature Vol.I Ed. by Eric Kraus

Street Talk: Character Monologues for Actors By Glenn Alterman

The Ultimate Audition Book: 222 Monologues, 2 Minutes & Under Ed. by Jocelyn A. Beard

The Ultimate Audition Book Vol.II: 222 Monologues, 2 Minutes & Under from Literature Ed. by John Capecci, Laurie Walker, and Irene Ziegler

The Ultimate Audition Book Vol.III: 222 Monologues, 2 Minutes & Under from the Movies Ed. by John Capecci, Laurie Walker, and Irene Ziegler

Uptown: Character Monologues for Actors By Glenn Alterman